Original title:
The Seahorse's Serenade

Copyright © 2025 Creative Arts Management OÜ
All rights reserved.

Author: Isabella Rosemont
ISBN HARDBACK: 978-1-80587-326-6
ISBN PAPERBACK: 978-1-80587-796-7

Secrets Among the Algae

In the green where critters giggle,
A seaweed party makes us wiggle.
The shrimp dance in a silly way,
While fish throw confetti to play.

Bubbles burst with a pop and a fizz,
As crabs strut like they're on a quiz.
Starfish wear hats, oh what a sight,
And seahorses twirl in pure delight.

Nautical Whispers of Affection

A puffer fish tries to blow a kiss,
But instead, it's a puff of abyss.
Octopus winks with eight folds of charm,
While jellyfish giggle, causing alarm.

Clownfish swim in a comical race,
With bubbles that pop, they abandon grace.
The turtles roll in a giggly heap,
As whales hum songs that cause fish to peep.

Chasing Shadows in the Seafoam

In frothy waves, shadows swirl,
As turtles chase each other in a twirl.
Dolphins play tag, it's quite a show,
While sea cucumbers steady and slow.

A lobster joins in, thinking he's sly,
With pinchers wide, he gives it a try.
The seagulls cackle, circling above,
As fish start mulling their underwater love.

Emotions in the Coral Abyss

In colors bright, the corals sway,
Fish express love in their own funky way.
A grouper blushes, a little shy,
While angelfish leap and flutter nearby.

The sea anemones share a tease,
With clownfish tangled, oh what a breeze!
Flirting in currents, they giggle and jest,
In the coral's embrace, they make love the best.

Reflections in the Bay

In a mirror of water, a fish takes a glance,
With a wink and a wiggle, it tries its best dance.
A crab claps along with a rhythm so bold,
While the octopus giggles, its secrets unfold.

The shrimp throw a party, oh what a delight,
With bubbles and sparkles, they twirl in the night.
But the goggle-eyed flounder just stares in surprise,
At the chaos of friends with their colorful ties.

Fluid Poetry of the Ocean

Waves whisper verses, a soft salty tune,
As jellyfish spin in a wiggly swoon.
The starfish all giggle, oh what a bright show,
While the seaweed sways in a rhythmic flow.

A clam plays the conch with a honk and a toot,
While the seashells giggle in sparkly loot.
The dolphins all leap in a splashing ballet,
While the krill tap their feet to the ocean's ballet.

The Deep's Gentle Caress

In the deep blue, the narwhal takes flight,
With its twisty horn, it dances with might.
The seahorses chuckle, in fancy old suits,
With tails all entwined, they wiggle their boots.

The snail's on a race, though it's taking a while,
While the guppies laugh hard, in a swirling pile.
A pufferfish blows up, all round and so neat,
Making everyone giggle, oh how sweet!

Tails of the Tidal Pool

In the rock pools, creatures all come out to play,
With sea stars and mackerel enjoying the ray.
A crab tries to dance but ends up in a flail,
While nudibranchs chuckle at the silly detail.

A jellyfish bobs like a bobbing balloon,
While the seagulls squawk in their silly tune.
The little fish flit with a flash and a dart,
In the tidal pool's laughter, they'll never depart.

Bedtime Ballads from Beneath

In the depths where shadows play,
Sea critters dance at end of day.
A fish in pajamas, oh what a sight,
Chasing glowing bubbles that burst with delight.

Octopus juggles shells with flair,
While clams snap shut with a silent glare.
Turtles in tuxedos swim in a race,
Laughing at seaweed caught on their face.

Squid plays the drums on a coral reef,
Sardines request a tune, quite brief.
Starfish claps with its five tiny arms,
While a crab shows off its quirky charms.

Dolphins flip in a giggly spree,
Making waves of laughter in the deep blue sea.
With tales of mischief and a splash of fun,
The underwater party has just begun!

Velvet Shadows of the Abyss

In velvet shadows, creatures roam,
A jellyfish floats like an underwater tome.
With neon lights that twinkle and gleam,
It's a psychedelic oceanic dream.

Gobies gossip, their chatter's a tease,
Whispering secrets to the gentle breeze.
With fish in wigs and a clownfish's grin,
A show down below where the fun begins!

An anglerfish boasts of its glowing lure,
While the eel just wiggles, unsure and unsure.
Pufferfish puff up, pretending to fright,
Who knew that the deep could be such a sight?

As they dance to the rhythm of the tide's sweet sway,
The ocean's humor brightens their way.
In the depths of the sea, laughter is king,
In the depths of the sea, come join and sing!

Aqua Vista Verses

In aqua vistas, fish take a leap,
Popping above for a giggle, not sleep.
A crab in a hat makes its way to the fair,
While seahorses twist without a care.

There's a whale with a horn, just blowing a tune,
While seagulls flap wings, crooning a swoon.
The starfish tells jokes to a gathering crowd,
Its humor so bright, it could make you loud!

Bubbles rise high as the clownfish does dance,
Swaying through currents, oh what a chance!
To sway like the kelp in the fresh ocean air,
Where laughter and joy have a casual flair.

So join in the fun, let your spirits be free,
In the charm of the waves, come and see!
With a splash and a giggle, the sea calls your name,
Keep swimming and shining, for it's all just a game!

Algae's Secret Song

In green disguise, they sway and play,
With tiny beats, they dance all day.
Each bubble pops, a giggle bursts,
A party hosted by the sea's first.

Underneath the ocean's glow,
Jellyfish join with a quirky show.
They twirl and dip, with a splash and a spin,
All while the fish just grin and grin.

Rhythm of the Rippled Waters

A crab in shades, tiptoes with flair,
While clams applaud from their sandy lair.
The rhythm flows in wobbly beats,
As seahorses hoof it on tiny feet.

Starfish cheer with a slow-motion clap,
While sea turtles nap in their cushy lap.
The waves make music, a splishy-splash,
As fish in tuxedos perform in a flash.

Sonnet of the Sea's Embrace

A seaweed joke floats by with a grin,
It tickles the fins of the fish within.
The waves grow bold, they throw a punch,
As dolphins leap, they gather for lunch.

A lobster winks with a little tease,
While octopuses juggle with effortless ease.
In this comic play under shimmering skies,
The ocean's mirth is a sweet surprise.

Harmony Beneath the Waves

Oh, what a ruckus beneath the foam,
As every critter claims their home.
A clownfish shouts with a nose so bright,
"Who tickled my tail? It's quite a sight!"

The barnacles chuckle, holding tight,
While pufferfish perform in delight.
With laughter shared across the sea,
All creatures join in the revelry.

A Symphony Beneath the Waves

In the depths where fish all dance,
A jaunty tune gives them a chance.
Crabs click-clack in time with glee,
A waltz of bubbles, oh so free.

Jellyfish jiggle, quite a sight,
They glide like stars, a pure delight.
Shrimps do a shifty little jig,
Who knew they were such stars, so big?

Octopuses hide, playing peek-a-boo,
With a shoe on a tentacle, it's quite the view!
The fish all chuckle as they swim around,
In this underwater circus, joy is found.

So come, let's groove beneath the sea,
Where every creature's a VIP.
A symphony of laughter, bright and bold,
In the ocean's heart, a story unfolds.

Floating Dreams of Aqua Bliss

In the currents, dreams take flight,
Bubbles pop with sheer delight.
A clownfish giggles, making faces,
As sea turtles join in playful races.

Starfish stretch on sandy beds,
Counting the waves with tiny heads.
A seagull drops a shiny shell,
"Oops, my talent is to fell!"

A dolphin's flip brings cheers from fish,
"Makin' waves is our only wish!"
They spin and splash, their laughter loud,
Making even the coral feel proud.

So float with us, in currents bright,
Where water sparkles, pure delight.
In dreams of aqua, fun and play,
A world of wonders leads the way.

Tango of Tails in Twilight's Glow

In twilight's glow, the ocean sways,
Creatures gather for a dance of days.
Seahorses twirl in fancy dress,
With tails intertwined, what a mess!

A crab taps feet upon the sand,
While a flounder tries to understand.
"Is it left, or is it right?"
Their goofy steps are quite a sight!

Bubblefish puff up, looking grand,
While shrimp do the cha-cha, oh so planned.
In every twist, and every whirl,
They laugh and giggle, what a swirl!

As the stars blink in the ocean's dome,
They dance the night, their watery home.
A tango of tails, a joyful show,
In the deep sea's arms, they steal the glow.

Echoes of a Sunlit Reef

In the reef where colors play,
Echoes bounce from here to stay.
A parrotfish, with jaw open wide,
Chomps on coral, full of pride.

"Now that's a crunch!" the sea fans cheer,
With every bite, they draw near.
A needlefish darts, moving quick,
"Look at me go! I'm quite the trick!"

Anemones dance, waving in delight,
As clownfish giggle, "We own the night!"
Coral formations sway in the tide,
To a melody, where all confide.

In the sunlit beauty, they all unite,
Laughing and playing, oh what a sight!
Echoes of laughter, bright and bold,
In the reef's embrace, their stories unfold.

Whispers of the Ocean's Dance

In the depths where light gets shy,
A fish tells jokes as bubbles fly.
With fins that flitter, they prance in glee,
While kelp sways along, just like a spree.

A crab wears a hat and struts with flair,
While clams clap shells, they cheer and care.
The starfish giggles, a ticklish delight,
As the sea turtles waltz through the night.

The jellyfish jive, swaying to the beat,
With squishy moves that can't be beat.
The whispering waves join in the fun,
As they laugh and dance 'til the day is done.

In the Embrace of Currents

With a flip and a flap, the minnows tease,
Swirling round like a laugh in the breeze.
They dart and they dive, a slippery show,
Making waves in a dance, oh what a blow!

An octopus grins, ink flinging wide,
It's a color explosion; it's its joyride.
The whales hum tunes, silly and grand,
While playful sea otters roll in the sand.

Fish fashionista, they strut with pride,
In shimmering scales, they can't help but glide.
With each splash and ripple, giggles abound,
In their watery world, joy is unbound.

Courtship Among Coral Gardens

In corals bright, the critters parade,
Bubbles of laughter, they serenade.
A pufferfish puffs, trying to impress,
While the clownfish dances, in a funny mess.

A shy little shrimp, with a wink and a nod,
Dances a jig on the back of a cod.
Sea cucumbers wave, not quite so spry,
While the anemones giggle, oh my, oh my!

As sea urchins scoff, they can't find their dance,
The group keeps on swirling in the romance.
A swish and a swash, the ocean's delight,
With partners galore, they dance through the night.

Marine Melodies of Love

In a bubbling tune, the flounders croon,
With voices like bubbles, they sing to the moon.
A herring whispers sweet fishy dreams,
While shrimp play guitar with their shellfish gleams.

The sea anemones sway with such grace,
Tickling the fins of a love-struck bass.
They twirl and they wink as sand pours like gold,
In this watery ballet, romance unfolds.

The sea stars shimmy in a shimmering line,
Spreading their joy like a glass of fine wine.
With each salty breeze, love wafts all around,
In the laughter of waves, true joy can be found.

Murmurs from the Marine Gardens

In gardens where the seaweed sways,
Fish gossip in the sun's bright rays.
A crab plays piano on a shell,
While jellyfish dance, oh so well!

Octopus juggles with bits of foam,
A ticklish tide feels right at home.
Starfish twirl like they own the place,
Laughter bubbles, a bubbly chase!

Seashell choirs sing in coral keys,
A dolphin giggles, smacks the seas.
They flip and flop in joyous cheer,
Making waves, spreading good vibes here!

Kelp swings high with a vibrant flair,
Tangled tales fill the salty air.
Who knew the sea could host such fun?
Underwater antics, never done!

Dreamweaver of the Blue

Bubbles float like dreams at play,
Octopus knots in a funny way.
Seahorses wear tuxedos tight,
Dancing under stars so bright!

Clown fish giggle in a parade,
Waving to fans, their fin-made trade.
The turtles slow-dance with a charm,
Bringing laughter, and no alarm!

Anemones bob like waving hands,
Creating tunes with seaweed bands.
Whales join in with a booming sound,
Making the ocean's joy profound!

Twilight whispers on waves so light,
Under the moon, all feels just right.
With every splash, a joke is made,
In this underwater masquerade!

The Lost Melodies of Molasses

Molasses flows in a sticky stream,
Crabs make music, or so it seems.
Gummy bears float with such delight,
In a candy sea that sparkles bright!

Fins shimmer like candy cane swirls,
While flounders share their fishy twirls.
Sardines hum a whimsical tune,
While seagulls croon beneath the moon!

Jellybeans bob on waves of fun,
To a syrup beat, they dance and run.
A turtle strums with sea-glass picks,
Gliding through endless ocean tricks!

Lost melodies, oh what a sight,
Playful nonsense in the night.
Every bubble giggles with glee,
In sweet, sticky harmony!

Eight-Legged Rhythms

Eight-legged wonders strut their show,
Dancing in circles, just like a pro.
With wiggly legs and a quirky sway,
They'll make you chuckle, come what may!

Squids stomp to a wobbly beat,
While shrimps join in, oh so neat!
Their tentacles swirl like ribbons bright,
Creating a spectacle, pure delight!

Clams clap shells in a rhythmic cheer,
Joining this jolly ocean sphere.
An octopus leads with rhythmic flair,
Bubbles burst like giggles in the air!

Under the waves, the party flows,
Where every creature hilarity sows.
In this dance, joy twines with bliss,
A funny frolic you shouldn't miss!

Celestial Chords of the Tide

In the deep, a fish can sing,
With a twirl and a joyful fling.
Crabs join in with a silly clap,
As waves lap up in a rhythmic tap.

Turtles groove on the ocean floor,
While sea cucumbers do adore!
Dolphins jump, they can't resist,
In this underwater music twist.

Starfish spin like a dance craze,
Swirling 'round in ocean haze.
With every splash, a laugh erupts,
As seagulls watch, their heads are cupped.

Octopuses play the bass so low,
Their eight arms sway, to and fro.
It's a concert beneath the brine,
Where every bubble contents divine!

Moonlit Melodies of the Aquatic Realm

Under the moon, the fish do prance,
Each one eager for a chance.
A clownfish jokes with a wink and grin,
Declaring, 'Let the fun begin!'

A starfish with a ukulele bright,
Strums silly songs under the night.
While jellyfish join with bioluminescent glow,
Their dance is quite the underwater show.

Pufferfish puffed up for the beat,
Blowing bubbles, oh what a treat!
A lobster laughs, his pinch not mean,
In this wild aquatic scene.

As the tide sways with playful cheer,
All the sea critters gather near.
With every splash, a chuckle shared,
A symphony of silly moments declared!

The Whispering Wandering Waves

Waves dance in with a giggling sound,
As fishy friends gather around.
A sea otter slips and slides,
In a game where fun never hides.

Barnacles tap their tiny feet,
Joining in on the rhythmic beat.
A fish wearing glasses, quite the sight,
Sends everyone into sheer delight!

With the current's squishy sway,
A playful clam says, 'Come out and play!'
Bubbles puff out with every tease,
As laughter floats upon the breeze.

Whispers of joy in the salty air,
Where even shy fishes learn to share.
A world of whimsy, singing bright,
With every wave, pure delight!

Secrets of the Sunken Garden

In a garden below the sea,
Where fish and weeds dance wild and free.
A crab tells tales of adventures bold,
Of treasures found and stories told.

Anemones twirl in vibrant attire,
With costumes made by the ocean's choir.
Seaweed sways with a giggly delight,
As creatures join in, oh what a night!

A fish in a crown, a real sight to see,
Proclaims, 'Join my kingdom, all are free!'
With bubbles rising in the warm tide,
Even shy snails take a joyful glide.

Underwater flavors fill the scene,
As parrotfish munch on veggies green.
In this sunken world, the laughter flows,
In a grand show where the fun just grows!

Currents of Ancient Stories

In the reef where fish adore,
A tale swims through the ocean floor.
With bubble laughs and flip-flop grace,
A seahorse prances, a silly race.

Old crabs scuttle with clanking claws,
While starfish cheer with many a pause.
The seaweed waves like it's in a dance,
Join the fun, take a silly chance!

Jellyfish jive, so wobbly and bright,
Tickled by currents that whisper delight.
A sea turtle smiles with a wink and a nod,
What a peculiar party, oh my, how odd!

As tides bring stories from far and wide,
Bubbles and giggles can't be denied,
In this underwater world full of glee,
Every creature laughs, how wild, oh wee!

The Gentle Tug of the Tide

With seaweed swaying to a merry tune,
The lobsters groove beneath the moon.
A seahorse trots in tiny shoes,
"Kick up your fins, we can't lose!"

A clam plays hide and seek in the sand,
While a shoal of fish forms a conga band.
They wiggle and giggle, it's quite a sight,
Underwater antics brought to light.

A crab invents a dance called the slide,
As dolphins twirl and take it in stride.
The waves chuckle, "What fun can we find?"
In this breezy ballet, all are intertwined.

With splashes of laughter and bubbles of cheer,
Every mollusk grins, no worry or fear.
As tides ebb and flow, here's the grand ride,
Together they play, side by side.

Enchantment Beneath the Sea

In a castle of coral, the prince lost his hat,
While seahorses giggle, "Look at that!"
Starfish clapped while clams would sing,
"Oh, what joy such a mishap can bring!"

A clownfish juggled some shiny pearls,
As anemones danced in a twist and swirls.
The octopus painted with colors so bright,
Turning sea-floor messes to whimsical light.

A dolphin spun like the whirling tide,
Splashing about with friends by his side.
Crabs played the drums, a crabby parade,
In this underwater world so cleverly made.

With whispers of fun in soft bubble tones,
A fest of laughter among the sea bones.
Beneath foam and froth, joy carries the plea,
"Life is a party, dance wild and free!"

Tidal Tones at Dusk

As daylight fades with a splash of red,
Seahorses gather their flowers of thread.
They hum a tune, silly and sweet,
Join in the fun, don't miss a beat!

The sea sponges giggle and tumble around,
Creating a ruckus, making a sound.
"Who stole my shell?" a hermit crab cries,
While the fish just chuckle, rolling their eyes.

Urchins are bouncing, what a sight to behold!
In waves they leap as the night grows bold.
Twinkling stars wink as sea critters sway,
With joyful hearts, they dance come what may.

At dusk's soft tide, laughter's the theme,
Swaying together like a watery dream.
In every splash, there's a shout and a cheer,
For life undersea is eternally clear!

Chiming Dreams of Dolphin Dances

In the sea where whales sing,
Dolphins twist in joyful fling.
Bubbles burst with giggles bright,
Flipping high, what a sight!

Turtles cheer from the sandy floor,
Clapping fins, they want to soar.
Jellyfish glow with laughter near,
Dancing waves, no room for fear.

Octopuses twirl, so deft and spry,
Throwing ink to paint the sky.
Every splash is met with glee,
Underwater jubilee.

A clownfish jokes with a wink and grin,
In this ocean fest, everyone wins.
As the sun sets, they take their bows,
Making ripples to share their vows.

Serenade of Aquatic Hues

Coral reefs hum a silly tune,
Starfish stomp to the bubble bassoon.
Colors dance like a painting bright,
Each shade twisting, pure delight.

Anemones sway, tickling fish,
Making friends is their only wish.
With every wave, a chuckle flows,
Together they share all their woes.

Pufferfish puff, trying to fright,
But while they swell, they lose their fight.
With a pop and a giggle spree,
They laugh and bounce, so wild and free.

In this watery carnival of cheer,
Every critter has a role here.
As laughter sings through the blue expanse,
They join the currents in a jolly dance.

Elysian Refrains of the Reef

Beneath the waves, a playful show,
Fish don costumes, a bright tableau.
With fins like ribbons and smiles galore,
They swirl around, shout for more!

A seahorse rides a bubble jet,
Spinning tales you won't forget.
Crabs tap dance on the ocean floor,
In this realm, who could ask for more?

A clam plays piano, so out of tune,
While shrimp bust moves to a catchy tune.
Whales hum harmonies, deep and true,
Creating giggles as they swim through.

As tides shift and laughter spreads,
Sea creatures dance on coral beds.
Each moment filled with a gleeful song,
In this vibrant world, we all belong.

The Ocean's Heartbeat

A wave crashes with a cheeky splash,
A surfboard rides in a gleeful flash.
Fish surf on bubbles, laughing aloud,
Joining the sea in currents proud.

Squids squirt ink in a playful game,
While grinning crabs look on, calling names.
Every leap is met with roars of fun,
In this marine party, no one's outdone.

Seals roll about, full of delight,
Juggling seaweed, oh what a sight!
A medley of laughter, all around,
In their ocean kingdom, joy is found.

As the sun dips low, they raise a cheer,
In salty air, there's nothing to fear.
For in this deep blue, together they play,
Creating memories that won't fade away.

A Waltz Through the Waves

In the ocean's grand ballet,
A fish wore a frilly bouquet.
He twirled with a grin,
His dance was a win,

With a jig and a spin,
He made all the critters grin.
The clam clapped with glee,
Said, "Join in, you'll see!"

Crabs tried to follow the beat,
But tripped over their own little feet.
They laughed as they stumbled,
In the waves, they tumbled.

With bubbles and laughs so bright,
Their waltz lit up the night.
A splash of pure fun,
For all, it was done.

Starlit Waters' Sweet Serenade

Under starlight, fish did sway,
Playing tunes in a silly way.
The octopus plucked strings,
While seahorses danced with bling.

A turtle chimed in with a beat,
Swishing sand with his happy feet.
The moonbeams started to twirl,
As waves giggled and would swirl.

"Let's coordinate our styles!"
Cried the dolphin, with playful smiles.
They jumped and they splashed,
With joy unabashed.

The jests of the sea rang loud,
Gathering every fishy crowd.
In laughter, they basked,
As the night blissfully passed.

Ethereal Dances of the Deep

In the depths where the bubbles bloom,
Creatures gather, dispelling gloom.
A shrimp led the breakdancing show,
With moves that made others go "Whoa!"

Twirling through kelp and driftwood,
Each twist brought giggles, oh, so good.
A blowfish puffed, then burst with a cheer,
"How about some fun over here?"

The anglerfish flashed a light,
Guiding the dancers through the night.
With flicks of their tails,
They created wild tales.

Together they spun and twined,
In a jest that was quite well-defined.
The ocean echoed their song,
Where all merry souls belong.

The Love Verses of the Tide

Amidst the waves, a romance brewed,
With fish declaring their love, quite crude.
"A heart-shaped shell is quite a catch!"
Said one guppy, with flair to match.

"Now, what do I wear?" a clownfish frets,
As anemones giggle with little bets.
"Just be yourself and have some fun!
Your stripes are perfect, you're number one!"

The jellyfish glided, lovey-dovey,
While sea urchins squabbled, feeling stuffy.
A crab threw a dance party, oh so bright,
Under the stars, on a magical night.

With flirty bubbles and playful winks,
Every sea creature made time to sync.
Laughter and love swirled in the tide,
In the grand ocean, joy was their guide.

Swirls in Twilight Waters

In the twilight waters, creatures prance,
A seahorse giggles with a sideways glance.
Bubbles rise up, tickling their fins,
As seaweed waltzes, a dance that wins.

Jellyfish jive with their glowing flair,
While crabs tap dance, without a care.
The clownfish chuckles, a fishy tale,
In these twilight waters, we all set sail.

Starfish are jugglers, spinning around,
While octopuses play with lost socks found.
The anemones giggle, swaying in rhyme,
Making waves with their flow, a slippery climb.

In laughter we swim, through sea and glee,
Twilight waters, forever carefree.
Where joy's a current, playful and bright,
Beneath the waves, pure delight takes flight.

Songbirds of the Seven Seas

In the ocean blue, where the fish croon,
Echoes of laughter, a bubbly tune.
Gulls try to sing but sound quite absurd,
While dolphins giggle, not a word heard.

The octopus strums with a slippery grace,
Twirling his tentacles, what a funny face!
Turtles are beatboxing, creating a show,
As sea anemones sway, putting on a glow.

With shells as drums, the clams go thump,
While sea urchins sway, giving a jump.
The starfish harmonize, a chorus so grand,
In the symphony of water, we take a stand.

Oh, songbirds of the seas, all take a bow,
With laughter and music, here and now.
Together we play, on this watery stage,
Crafting our joy, like a good-natured sage.

Liquid Love Letters

In swirling tides, secrets float and spin,
With liquid love letters tucked deep within.
Gifts from the reef, wrapped in a smile,
As fish deliver jokes, swimming a mile.

Seashells whisper sweet nothings aloud,
While bubbles pop merrily, drawing a crowd.
The pufferfish puffs, a comedian's flair,
As the angelfish laughs, caught unaware.

The tides bring tales, written in sand,
Filled with puns that are simply grand.
In this ocean of laughter, we send our affection,
With joyful splashes, a quirky connection.

So dive into depths where giggles abide,
In liquid love letters, let joy be our guide.
With silliness swirling, a tide of delight,
In the heart of the ocean, everything's bright.

Ink of the Ocean's Heart

Beneath the waves, with pen and quill,
The ocean writes stories that give us a thrill.
Ink flows like currents, each tale a delight,
As fish share their secrets in the moonlight.

Crabs draft amusing plays, full of quirks,
While schools of fish perform silly works.
The sea turtle scribbles, slow but sure,
In the ink of the ocean, humor is pure.

Squids write love letters, with their squiggly style,
While starfish play editors, all the while.
Whales sing sonnets, rich with charm,
Inking our hearts, with their ocean alarm.

So gather your stories, let laughter take flight,
In the ocean's heart, everything feels right.
With ink that flows freely, we blend and we part,
Binding our joy in the ocean's heart.

Choreography of the Chromatic Fish

Bubbles pop in playful dance,
The fish twirl in a vibrant prance.
Colors splash like paint, a show,
Who knew fish could steal the flow?

A clownfish jokes, a jester bright,
Tickling fins and laughing light.
Tangles of seaweed join the spree,
Even crabs clack their claws with glee.

Driftwood waltzes, sways with pride,
While otters spin and glide beside.
In this ocean's merry stage,
A comedy that won't age.

And with each flip and cheeky grin,
A bubble chorus can begin.
The sea's a laugh, a frolicking dish,
Who knew fish could be this delish?

Waltz of the Water's Edge

At the shore where the seaweed sings,
The sea stars practice silly flings.
Tidepools mimic a dance of glee,
As creatures shimmy, wild and free.

Shells wear pearls like crowns on heads,
Crabs do the moonwalk, like it spreads.
Gulls giggle and join in the fun,
Pecking the sand, under the sun.

A jellyfish glides with a jiggle,
While seagulls dance and give a wiggle.
Each wave rolls in with a chuckle,
Spreading joy without a struggle.

In this tide of mirth and play,
Every splash brings laughter's way.
Oh, the antics that life can stage,
At the beach, a whimsical page!

Sonorous Secrets of the Abyss

Down where the shadows dance and glide,
Whispers of laughter try to hide.
An anglerfish winks with his light,
Drawing in friends for a good-night sight.

Octopus games, like hide and seek,
Changing colors with each little peek.
They jest with charm, ten arms at play,
It's a circus, a nightly ballet.

Even the clams can't resist the fun,
Snapping shells like a drumbeat run.
Eels poke their heads, join the plight,
Grooving along to the sound of night.

A symphony deep, with giggles galore,
Where fish pass by, with tales to explore.
In the murky depths, hilarity flows,
Secrets of joy, as the ocean knows.

Ballad of the Brine

In briny depths, a tale unfurls,
With fish in hats and seaweed curls.
A walrus played a saxophone,
Echoes of laughter, everywhere blown.

The sea turtles dance with twirling shells,
While dolphins laugh like ringing bells.
A crab recites poetry quite bold,
While shrimp and scallops glimmer like gold.

Beneath the waves, a party brews,
With seashells rattling their lively views.
As bubbles pop and jellyfish glide,
The ocean's secrets, a joyful ride.

In this ballad sung by salty foam,
Creatures gather, calling it home.
For in the brine, laughter will reign,
A melody of cheer, like summer rain.

Nautical Nocturne

In the deep blue, a dance takes place,
With fish in tuxedos, all full of grace.
Octopus plays the piano with ease,
While clams clap along, swaying in the breeze.

Jellyfish glow like disco balls,
Seahorses twist and spin in the halls.
They giggle and wiggle, what a delight,
As the starfish joins in, shining so bright.

A crab with a hat starts tapping his feet,
While shrimp in a line boast their spicy beat.
The eels make a slinky, sliding along,
Singing silly tunes, all feeling so strong.

In this watery world, no need for a shore,
The bubbles are giggling, who could want more?
With every splash, a new laugh is shared,
This oceanic party, no one is spared.

Fluid Dreams of the Deep

In the sea where the currents twirl,
A fish in a top hat begins to whirl.
Turtles spin tales of adventures wide,
While blennies slide by with unending pride.

The stingrays glide in their graceful flight,
Making shapes in the sand, what a sight!
Clownfish tell jokes, tickled by glee,
As seaweed sways like a carefree tree.

Anemones chuckle, swaying around,
While seafans flutter, making soft sound.
A dolphin breaks in with a splashy dash,
His flips and tricks, a glittering flash.

As bubbles rise up, with giggles they flee,
Each wave brings laughter, as light as can be.
In dreams of the ocean, a carnival reigns,
With funny friends dancing, where humor remains.

Serenade of the Serpent Sea

In the depths where the sea serpents glide,
Bubbles burst forth, and laughter can't hide.
A narwhal pops out, a hat on his horn,
Making all fish giggle, from dusk until morn.

Eels twist about, with a shimmy and shake,
Creating a rhythm, no chance they'll break.
Starfish do cartwheels, bright as can be,
While the clownfish are chuckling, filled with glee.

The lanternfish glitter with stories to share,
Of shipwrecks and treasure and the wild they dare.
An octopus joins, with eight arms in the air,
Telling jokes that swirl round in the salty air.

With the swish and the splash, fun flows like a stream,
The ocean's a stage, where everything's a dream.
In this serpent sea, no burden can weigh,
Just laughter and music, all night and all day.

Vibrations of the Ocean Floor

Down deep where the sand whispers sweet,
Crabs play maracas with shell-clad feet.
The sea cucumbers groove in the tide,
Offering snickers, all comfy inside.

With conch shells playing tunes from afar,
The fish all assemble, what a bizarre!
A parade of the goofy, in colors so bold,
With stories of mischief and treasures untold.

Seahorses prance in their elaborate suits,
While clams tell their secrets in hushed, silly hoots.
Mollusks spin tales, with a howl and a cheer,
Creating a vibe that draws everyone near.

In the symphony deep, waves giggle and soar,
Each ripple's a note that connects to the core.
So laugh with the tide and let worries be swayed,
In the ocean's deep song, all fun is displayed.

The Ballet of Fins and Waves

In the ocean's grand performance,
Fins flap like dancers in a trance.
They twist and whirl with joyful grace,
Making waves while they prance.

A starfish plays the maracas,
While seaweed sways in time.
A crab rolls by with a funny hat,
Saying, 'Hey there, it's mime!'

Jellyfish glide with grace untold,
Bouncing to a rhythm near the reef.
They float like balloons in colors bold,
Causing fish to laugh in disbelief.

The shellfish troupe takes center stage,
Snapping claws in a grand display.
With every wave, they steal the show,
At the ocean's theater, night and day.

Colorful Chronicles of the Coast.

On the beach, where colors clash,
A parrotfish writes tales in the sand.
With every flick of its vibrant tail,
It strikes a pose, oh isn't it grand?

The hermit crab has new digs today,
In a shiny shell that sparkles bright.
He struts about, saying, 'Look at me!'
While seagulls cackle in delight.

A curious octopus does a jig,
In hues of purple and green delight.
He twirls and sways, so slick and big,
Leaving fish to laugh at the sight.

And as the sun sets on this funny tale,
The waves echo laughter, soft and free.
For every creature, without fail,
Finds joy in the coast's bright spree.

Ocean Whispers

In the quiet deep, the fish huddle close,
Whispering secrets, giggles abound.
A shrimp believes it's a famous host,
Telling tales without making a sound.

An anemone hears them all quite well,
Chiming in with a rustling laugh.
"Join us for tea," it says with a swell,
"Just don't mind the bubbles from my staff!"

A turtle rolls by, sporting a grin,
Saying, "I'm late for my shellfish spree!"
Dancing with sea slugs, wide as a pin,
While coral reefs sing in harmony.

As currents carry their whispers afar,
The ocean chuckles and sways with glee.
For in this watery world, bizarre,
All creatures share their funny decree.

Dance of the Gentle Currents

The currents sway with a playful nudge,
Inviting the fish to come out and play.
They swirl and dive, with no need to judge,
Chasing bubbles that giggle away.

A flounder hides in the sandy floor,
"Where's my dance partner?" it cries with a joke.
A clownfish replies from behind a door,
"Just flipping the beats, now that's how I poke!"

An eel does tricks, all tangles and spins,
While a pufferfish blows up with delight.
They're playing a game, as the laughter begins,
With the sea as their stage for the night.

Together they move in a goofy ballet,
Chasing the tides 'til the morning light.
In oceans where laughter is here to stay,
Every creature joins in the fun and delight.

Poetry Among the Anemones

In gardens where the soft waves dance,
Anemones sway, they take a chance.
A crab with glasses reads a book,
While starfish gossip with a wink and look.

Bubble-blowing fish try to rhyme,
With quirky tunes, they spend their time.
A turtle twirls in a silly spree,
As colors swirl, just wait and see.

A clam attempts a joke so grand,
But slips and falls right on the sand.
The seaweed giggles in delight,
As laughter bubbles through the night.

So when you dive into the sea,
Remember all the joy and glee.
Among those blooms where giggles grow,
Funny tales of the tide's tableau.

Murmurs of the Ocean Floor

Beneath the waves where secrets creep,
The fish start murmuring, not a peep.
A snail with dreams of being fast,
Wonders if one day he'll be outclassed.

Crabs making jokes that pinch just right,
With every chuckle, they hold on tight.
An octopus juggles shells with flair,
While clams clap shells, trying to share.

In this realm of oddities and cheer,
A dolphin's giggle you can hear.
With fins that shiver from laughing so,
Each wave brings fun to their seaside show.

They dance and swirl, a playful crew,
Creating mirth with every hue.
So listen closely to the floor below,
For tales of giggles in ebb and flow.

Blissful Bubbles and Hidden Treasures

Bubbles float like dreams so light,
Underwater jesters take to flight.
A pufferfish blows up for a laugh,
While a dolphin stars in a comedy half.

Mermaids sing tunes with a wry twist,
As sea cucumbers make a list.
Of treasures found in giggles and glee,
Shells that shuffle, just wait and see.

In the deep where the corals play,
An eel tells tales that go astray.
While little fish swim by with glee,
Joining in on the underwater spree.

So come and join this splashy quest,
Where laughter reigns and all's the best.
Among the bubbles and treasures rare,
Giddy fun fills the salty air.

Currents of Passion in the Deep

Amidst the waves where currents tangle,
A starry-eyed fish starts to wrangle.
With dreams of love, she seeks her mate,
Hoping to find that special fate.

A grouper grins with a sly little glance,
As sea turtles join in the dance.
"Let's throw a party," they now declare,
With disco balls hanging everywhere.

The jellyfish glow as they flutter 'round,
Stirring the passion in the depths profound.
A lobster claps in colorful style,
As laughter echoes in every mile.

In the embrace of the ocean's call,
Where everyone's invited, one and all.
So swim along as the currents sweep,
And find love's laughter buried deep.

Dance of the Delicate Fin

In the coral sway they jig,
With tails that twist and a little gig,
Bubbles burst in a frothy cheer,
Who knew fish danced with such flair?

A jellyfish joins, wobbles around,
In a swaying rhythm, no feet on the ground,
Giggling clams clap their tiny shells,
While they spin in circles, casting spells.

An octopus prances, not missing a beat,
With tentacles flailing, oh what a feat!
Underwater rave, bubbles to the top,
Even the starfish can't help but bop!

So come join the bash in the sea's delight,
Where fish wear smiles and dance through the night,
A merry parade of fins and glee,
In this underwater jamboree!

The Soft Call of the Coast

Whispers of waves tickle the shore,
Crabs in a conga line, no need to implore,
Barnacles chat on the rocks they cling,
While the sea breeze hums a playful fling.

A pelican dives for a pastry treat,
Misses the splash, oh what a feat!
Seashells laugh, they'd roll on the sand,
If only they had a pair of hands.

Turtles play tag with drifting foam,
Squirting water, they feel right at home,
Seagulls squawk out their silly tune,
While flip-flops dance, who knew that they'd swoon?

So stroll to the rhythm where laughter is framed,
With nature's orchestra, no two days are same,
A soft call beckons, come join the fun,
At the coast where joyous moments run!

Ballad of the Bubble Life

Bubbles bounce in a shimmering spree,
Pop! says one, come dance with me!
Riding the currents, they float and glide,
With a giggle or two, there's nothing to hide.

Fish parade with a bubble hat,
Looking quite dapper, imagine that!
Each little puff is a joyous friend,
In this bubbly game that will never end.

A clownfish juggles, with a splash and a twirl,
While seaweed sways in a playful whirl,
Every bubble bursts in a giggly cheer,
Their laughter echoes as we draw near.

So come join the dance where bubbles convene,
In a watery party, a sight to be seen,
A ballad of joy beneath the bright light,
In the bubble life, let's revel tonight!

Rhapsody of Aquatic Breezes

Under the waves where the giggles play,
The fish make jokes in a splashy ballet,
Seahorses sport funny little ties,
While clownfish chuckle and roll their eyes.

A starfish recites some corny lines,
While the crabs throw in their best punchlines,
Turtles chuckle with shells all aglow,
As currents giggle, "Here we go!"

A dolphin dives with a wink and a spin,
In the rhapsody where laughter begins,
With every wave that breaks on the shore,
Joy bubbles up for us to explore.

So dive into this jesting embrace,
Where the sea's a riot, a whimsical place,
With dances and jokes to put you at ease,
In the breezes of laughter, let's ride the seas!

Echoes of the Eddying Foam

Bubbles rise with giggles loud,
A fish parade, oh what a crowd!
They twirl and dance in wavy grace,
Clownfish smile, what a funny face!

Seashells clap like tiny hands,
Joined by crabs in wiggly bands.
The octopus tells silly jokes,
While sea turtles share their pokes!

Dolphins leap with playful flair,
Spinning tales beyond compare.
Even the starfish join the show,
With silly moves, they steal the flow!

As twilight glints on waves so bright,
The ocean laughs into the night.
With echoes sweet and frothy cheer,
The sea's own song is loud and clear!

Harmonies of Salt and Sand

Sandy toes dance to the beat,
As gulls create a chirpy tweet.
Crabs dig holes where dreams can hide,
In salty grooves, they wiggle and slide!

Seagulls swoop with comic flair,
Stealing snacks without a care.
The seaweed sways with thoughts so green,
A jester's hat, what a sight seen!

In the tide pools, laughter echoes,
Anemones pull pranks, oh how it shows!
The sea cucumbers play dead,
While fish flip and tease instead!

As sunbeams dance on ocean's skin,
Puffers puff with goofy grin.
With every wave that curls and bends,
The ocean's humor never ends!

Poems of the Sacred Reef

Coral castles rise from deep,
Where sea creatures laugh and leap.
The parrotfish, with colors bold,
Tells tales of treasure chests of gold!

The lionfish flaunts its spiky hair,
As shrimp perform a tap dance, rare.
A starry night with fishy sights,
Crickets chirp in funny flights!

Seashells gather for a play,
In bubbles, they rehearse the day.
With underwater wiggles and flips,
The reef is alive with smiles and quips!

And when the moon pulls tides so high,
The reef erupts, oh my, oh my!
Laughter echoing, bright and free,
In this watery comedy!

Whispered Wishes in the Waters

Nudibranchs whisper silly dreams,
While playful waves burst at the seams.
A flounder hides in plain old sight,
While jellyfish float, oh what a sight!

Fiddler crabs strut, a flashy crew,
In sandy suits of shimmering hue.
The puffer fish pumps, a balloon at play,
As laughter bubbles up from the bay!

Tide pools giggle with critters shy,
As sea urchins poke, oh me, oh my!
Waves tickle rocks with bubbly laughs,
The ocean's a stage for its comical casts!

With moonlight casting shimmering trails,
The world beneath sings funny tales.
Each ripple, a twist on what will be,
In the deep blue, so wild and free!

Underwater Lullaby

In the depths where fish do dance,
A starfish twirls in a silly prance.
Bubble blowers laugh and cheer,
As clownfish wiggle, spreading cheer.

Octopus plays the ukulele,
Jellyfish sway, feeling gayly.
The seaweed sways, a dancer's friend,
As laughter echoes, the fun won't end.

Seahorses giggle in sleepy delight,
While crabs do cartwheels, what a sight!
Turtles wear hats, oh what a show,
In this underwater circus, let's go slow!

Starry nights above, the moonlight glows,
While fishies whisper all their woes.
The tides sing softly, a playful tune,
In dreams of bubbles, we drift by noon.

Coral's Sweet Symphony

In a reef where colors burst,
A trumpetfish plays, it's quite the first.
With seahorses lining up in rows,
Each takes a turn, and the rhythm grows.

Clownfish giggle, doing flips,
while sea cucumbers dance on tips.
Anemones wave their fluffy arms,
As everyone basks in aquatic charms.

A dolphin teacher leads the tune,
While crabs tapdance under the moon.
Each bubble pops, a note in the air,
Turns this symphony with flair and care.

Seashells clap with playful grace,
As eels slither, a rhythmic race.
Laughter rings through aquatic bliss,
Dancing together, we share a kiss!

Tales from the Tides

In the kelp forest, creatures tell,
Of mischief played by the clams so swell.
A seagull drops a sandwich near,
With fishy tales that bring us cheer.

Hermit crabs switch their shells so fine,
While shrimps sneak peeks—oh hey, that's mine!
Each story shared, a giggle's burst,
Pufferfish giggles, oh how they thirst!

Dancing with dolphins in a grand parade,
While stingrays glide, in sync, they wade.
An octopus spins yarns with a wink,
As turtles nod along, but think—

"Is this real?" they ponder and sway,
As fish fill the air with laughter's play.
The tides keep the stories flowing bright,
With every wave, a new delight.

Melody of the Marine Spirits

Under the sea, where voices chime,
With sea stars sprouting funky rhyme.
An old crab grumbles with a grin,
While minnows gather, ready to begin.

A walrus picks up a flute to play,
As guppies leap, in grand ballet.
The coral reef sways in the beat,
With every note, they shuffle their feet.

An echo of laughter breaks through the dance—
As flounders flop with silly advance.
The narwhals join, sharp horns in sight,
With every swish, they shine so bright.

In the depths, where the laughter flows,
Marine spirits sprinkle joy like snow.
Through bubbles and waves, a tale we weave,
In this silly dance, we'll never leave!

Tides of Forgotten Lore

In a tide pool, crabs juggle,
While starfish play humble pie.
A clam sings off-key, quite rude,
As seaweed dances, oh my!

Jellyfish wear hats made of foam,
While snails slide on slippery trails.
An octopus plays the trombone,
Bubbles burst like fishy tales.

Barnacles hold a talent show,
With oysters strumming seaweed strings.
Turtles cheer from the front row,
As laughter in the sea springs!

So if you roam the ocean's floor,
And hear giggles from afar,
Remember, the depths hold much more,
Than just sea life; they're a bizarre!

Starlit Soiree of the Sea

At midnight, the fish start to twirl,
With glowing scales, they take flight.
Anemones swirl and swirl,
Beneath the moon, oh so bright!

Seahorses in tuxedos, quite chic,
Spin like dancers on the floor.
A clownfish throws confetti, unique,
As dolphins sing, wanting more.

Starfish are the judges tonight,
With a score of bubbly glee.
They squeal at all the comical sights,
In this ocean jubilee!

So, come join this watery spree,
Where laughter is the main dish.
Beneath the waves, wild and free,
Life serves up an oceanic wish!

Fables from the Foam

Once a crab, with a top hat grand,
Declared he'd rule the coral reef.
But a seagull, with a snooty hand,
Laughing, brought him to grief.

A grouper told tales of great delight,
How he swam a thousand leagues.
But the truth? He fled from a fright,
Chased by curious sea leagues!

The wise old turtle, with a grin,
Announced a race with a big splash.
But the fish said, 'Oh no, we can't win,
We'd all end up in a mash!'

In the foam where fables are spun,
Laughter echoes, bright and clear.
Every creature joins in the fun,
And swims off without a fear!

Mare Nostrum Melodies

In the depths, a band of jelly,
Plays a tune that tickles the sea.
With each wiggle, the water's belly,
Shakes and bubbles with glee!

Clownfish, with their vibrant hue,
Tap dance on the coral's gate.
A grouch of a shark shouts, 'How rude!'
But all it does is contemplate.

The sea cucumbers join in the cheer,
Wobbling like they're in a trance.
They sway to the beat, it's quite sincere,
And coax the sea turtles to dance!

So gather near this watery show,
Where laughter flows like the tide.
In the Mare Nostrum, joy can grow,
And each creature takes great pride!

Golden Notes of Sunrise Splash

In the morning sun, a fish did prance,
With fins like ribbons, it took a chance.
It spun and twirled, danced with a grin,
Splashing the waves, where fun begins.

Bubbles burst with giggles and cheer,
As clams clapped shells, an audience here.
With jellyfish wiggling in their delight,
They laughed at the seagrass, a curious sight.

The starfish joined in, with arms all splayed,
Wiggling about, in a bright charade.
The ocean's laughter echoed all around,
As waves tickled toes, a joy newly found.

So when the tide comes rolling in,
Remember the dance and winsome grin.
Nature's stage is set for play,
Join in the fun, come splash, hooray!

Symphony of the Seashell

A cantata played by one brave clam,
With a gurgling sound and a bubbly slam.
The shells brought instruments, rocks sang low,
A symphony formed deep where sea currents flow.

The conch trumpet blared, a bold, loud sound,
While tiny sea anemones swayed all around.
Each wave noted rhythms of laughter and glee,
As crustaceans danced wildly with giddiness free.

A band of fish led the merry parade,
They flapped their tails in a funky charade.
The sea cucumbers, in their still fashion,
Wiggled along, causing quite a raction!

So next time you stroll past the shore,
Listen close for the music in the ocean's roar.
Feel the rhythm beneath your feet,
Where seashells join in, a tune so sweet!

Enchanted Echoes of the Expanse

In a world of bubbles, a fish did sing,
Tales of adventure, a bright fin-cling.
Echoes of laughter danced with the tide,
Joining the party, nature's wild ride.

The octopus played, with arms in a twist,
Creating a whirlpool, oh, what a twist!
Clownfish swirled, with colors so bright,
It turned into chaos, a cheeky delight!

Each creature within took turns to star,
The anglerfish lighting up from afar.
Seahorses giggled, in double time spins,
As turtles joined in, adding to grins.

So remember this show, each gurgle and cheer,
The ocean's a place where joy is clear.
With each wave that crashes upon the sand,
Comes laughter and fun, a sea-band so grand!

Secret Ballet of the Brackish

In waters where sweet and salty collide,
A hidden ballet, where critters abide.
The shrimp danced lightly with a pirouette,
While frogs croaked loudly, a jovial duet.

Dragonflies zoomed, like dancers on air,
With graceful flutters, they twirled without care.
Meanwhile, the mudskippers hopped with style,
In muddy old sneakers that made them worthwhile.

The reeds swayed gently, keeping time,
As the sun performed in rhythm and rhyme.
In rippling performances all around,
Laughter and splashes, the best magic found!

So join in the fun, let your spirits fly,
In hidden lagoons, beneath the vast sky.
For every splash carries stories untold,
In the secret ballet, where laughter unfolds!

Floating Fantasies Above

In the bubble of salt and glee,
A fish wears a hat, just like me.
They dance in the sea, so carefree,
Making bubbles for all to see.

The jellyfish jiggles, what a sight!
With tentacles swinging left and right.
A crab walking sideways, pure delight,
While sea turtles glide in the moonlight.

Starfish stars in the ocean's play,
Each twinkle whispers, "Come out and sway!"
With laughter echoing night and day,
This underwater ball is here to stay.

As waves roll in, a giggling game,
A dolphin jumps, calling each name.
In this watery world, never the same,
Life's a splash, join the wild fame!

Reverie of the Raging Waves

Oh, what fun in the swirling tide,
Where octopuses play and fish collide.
With fins all flapping, they take a ride,
In this merry surf, they won't hide.

A seal on a surfboard catches some rays,
Giggling and splashing in silly displays.
Waves wave back in comical ways,
As sea life dances, brightening the days.

A crab holds a shell, a fanciful hat,
'Tis a party down here, imagine that!
With squid paintbrushes, they make art splat,
On coral canvases— how about that?

Through rolling tides and frothy spins,
Creatures join in, their laughter begins.
Through salty dreams, let the fun never thin,
In this playful sea, everybody wins!

Chronicles of the Crashing Surf

In the heart of the surf, stories unfold,
Where sea cows wear glasses and don hats bold.
They gossip and giggle, secrets retold,
Of pirate gold and adventures of old.

The fish wear tuxedos, all so refined,
While sea urchins twist in the waves, intertwined.
A dance-off ensues, oh how they grind,
As laughter erupts, leaving worries behind.

A lobster tries salsa, a classic mistake,
With sideways shuffles, the crowd starts to quake.
The sea cucumbers cheer, never vague,
As mermaids make waves, for fun's own sake.

From bubbles like champagne to stories that twirl,
Each splash a delight in this water world swirl.
In the chronicles told with laughter to unfurl,
Every tide brings joy, and every wave a pearl!

Threads of Hope in the Ocean's Weave

Through the net of tides, adventures are spun,
With laughter that echoes, a joyous run.
Crabs having races, oh what fun,
As bubbles rise high under the sun.

A world of bright colors, where fish go to prance,
On seaweed dance floors, they twist and they glance.
With conch-shell trumpets, they all take a chance,
In this watery wonderland, a silly romance.

The anemone winks, it's a playful tease,
Swaying like dancers in the ocean breeze.
As clownfish giggle, they're sure to appease,
In this fibrous weave, laughter brings ease.

From coral to kelp, all having a blast,
Creating a tapestry, hilarity cast.
With the sea's laughter echoing, unsurpassed,
Hope is a thread that forever holds fast!

A Breeze Through the Ocean Wastes

A fish in a bowler hat, dancing with flair,
Swirls through the bubbles, without a care.
Crabs in a conga line wave with delight,
While turtles in shades groove into the night.

Jellyfish doing the moonwalk, how grand,
Pufferfish puffing, a night on the sand.
Clams clink their shells in a rhythmic pose,
As seagulls fulfill their comedy prose.

Octopus juggles seashells, oh what fun!
While dolphins flip-flop, oh look, they're done!
Anemones laugh with tentacles swayed,
In the dance of the sea, there's never dismayed.

A breeze whispers secrets, so silly, so sweet,
In the depths of the sea, the joy can't be beat.
A carnival underwater, all come to play,
With critters of nature who brighten the day.

Serenade of the Saltwater

The sea otter slides, with a wink and a grin,
Singing to starfish, inviting them in.
A crab tries to tango, but steps on a fin,
While sea cucumbers giggle at the din.

Bubbles pop rhythmically, a seaweed jig,
As dolphins make beats, with a flip and a swig.
Clownfish wear costumes, oh what a sight,
With wigs made of kelp, they dance with pure delight.

Barnacles cheer as the tide rolls along,
With a chorus of scallops, they sing their song.
An underwater party, so lively and free,
In saltwater serenades, all creatures agree.

Laughing and splashing, the waves have a say,
In the rhythm of water, they frolic and play.
With sea stars applauding, they steal the scene,
Life in the ocean, a true comic routine.

Chorus of the Coral Kingdom

In coral cities, the fish have a blast,
Where every bright color is made to outlast.
Sea horses strum seashells, a band on the go,
With clownfish as soloists, stealing the show.

Anemones sway to a quirky old tune,
As eels do the shimmy beneath the full moon.
Starfish cheer on in a light-hearted way,
As laughter bubbles up like a bright spray.

Moray eels linger, quite shy to the core,
While angelfish gossip, then ask for encore.
A parrotfish fluffs its bright, colorful scales,
As they all share their tales of exciting new trails.

The coral chorus, a sight to behold,
Where every sea creature shares stories untold.
In a kingdom so vivid, where joy never fades,
Underwater life dances, in shimmering shades.

Guardians of the Green Abyss

In the depths of green, where giggles reside,
Are guardians of laughter, with jokes they provide.
A turtle named Timmy, slow but so wise,
Tells tales of the sea with sparkles in his eyes.

A group of small fishes, all dressed up in style,
Sporting hats made of kelp, they swim for a while.
While crabs crack up jokes, but no one gets caught,
In their great little world, giggles won't rot.

Giant squids drawing mustaches in sand,
Making friends with the fish, they all join the band.
With laughter and bubbles, they twirl and they spin,
Sardines in a whirlpool, oh where to begin?

The guardians sing hymns, in a watery dome,
Reminding all creatures, the sea is their home.
With chuckles and cheer, they float 'neath the waves,
In the green abyss, where hilarity saves.

Glistening Echoes of the Blue

In ocean's dance, bubbles fly,
A fish tried to sing, oh my, oh my!
With a gurgle and splash, he lost his tune,
And echoed funny just like a cartoon.

A crab clapped along with a pinch-pinch sound,
While jellyfish laughed, swaying round and round.
Seahorses twirled, with a wink and a grin,
Their silly performances made the waves spin.

A turtle tapped along with his shell,
Turning a party into a swell.
The dolphins chuckled, spinning with flair,
In this wacky chorus, joy filled the air.

With a wink and a nod, the sea critters held,
A concert so quirky, no one repelled.
Underwater giggles danced through the tide,
In glistening echoes, the laughter did glide.

A Romance in the Seagrass

In seagrass fields where romance blooms,
A couple of shrimp made plans in the glooms.
She tossed him a wink, her antennae a-flutter,
He tripped on a shell, face first in the clutter.

Glimmers of sunlight danced on their heads,
While an octopus laughed from his cozy beds.
With each little blunder, love grew more strong,
They played a sweet tune to a jazzy sea song.

Nearby, clams clanked to the rhythm and beat,
While seagulls above cheered with flappy feet.
Shellfish couples slow danced, quite out of time,
As a lobster proposed with a seaweed rhyme.

Amidst all the laughter, they found their way,
In a wacky love story, beneath skies of gray.
With bubbles and giggles, they sealed their fate,
An adorable romance, quite simply first rate.

Serenading Underwater Starlight

Beneath the waves where stars twinkle bright,
A fish with grand hope sang into the night.
His voice like a trumpet, or so he believed,
But the bubbles that popped were what everyone received.

The seahorses snickered, their tails in a spin,
As he flailed his fins, trying hard to fit in.
With a splash and a giggle, they joined in the fun,
A chorus of laughter brought joy to everyone.

A dolphin dove deep, playing catch with a ray,
While a flounder flipped pancakes for the dance display.
Squid held confetti, painting the scene,
Under twinkling waters, all merry and keen.

As starfish twirled, the seaweed did sway,
In a wobbly rhythm, they brightened the day.
With a jubilant echo, the ocean did sing,
In this funny ballet, oh, what joy it did bring!

Whimsy of the Gently Drifting

Drifting along where the seaweed enthralls,
A sea cucumber tried to engage in some brawls.
With a squishy little body and quite the bold stare,
He went for a challenge, but forgot he was bare.

A pufferfish giggled, all puffed-up with pride,
As around him, the clownfish took a wild ride.
With antics delightful, they twirled and they flipped,
In the kooky underwater, not one wobbler slipped.

An urchin dressed up in a bright pumpkin hat,
Spinning and twisting, how silly was that?
They chuckled and danced, producing a show,
Of whimsy and fun in the soft current flow.

With coral confetti showering down,
The fish put on smiles, and they sparkled around.
In this floating circus, filled with delight,
Humor and joy made the dark sea seem bright.

www.ingramcontent.com/pod-product-compliance
Lightning Source LLC
Chambersburg PA
CBHW070005300426
43661CB00141B/250